THE PRINTING PRESS

Richard and Louise Spilsbury

Chicago, Illinois

www.heinemannraintree.com
Visit our website to find out
more information about
Heinemann-Raintree books.

To order:

☎ Phone 888-454-2279

🖥 Visit www.heinemannraintree.com
to browse our catalog and order online.

© 2012 Heinemann Library
an imprint of Capstone Global Library, LLC
Chicago, Illinois

Edited by Louise Galpine and Laura Knowles
Designed by Philippa Jenkins
Illustrations by KJA-artists.com
Original illustrations © Capstone Global Library
    Limited 2012
Picture research by Mica Brancic
Originated by Capstone Global Library Limited
Printed and bound in China by CTPS

15 14 13 12 11
10 9 8 7 6 5 4 3 2 1

Library of Congress Cataloging-in-Publication Data
Spilsbury, Richard, 1963-
    The printing press / Richard and Louise Spilsbury.
        p. cm.—(Tales of invention)
    Includes bibliographical references and index.
    ISBN 978-1-4329-4876-4 (hc)—ISBN 978-1-4329-
4885-6 (pb) 1. Printing—History—Juvenile literature.
2. Printing presses—History—Juvenile literature. I.
Spilsbury, Louise. II. Title.
    Z124.S74 2012
    686.2'09—dc22   2010036493

Acknowledgments
We would like to thank the following for permission
to reproduce photographs: Corbis pp. **4** (© Fine Art
Photographic Library), **8** (epa/© STR), **11** (Sygma/© Rick
Maiman), **15** (© Bettmann), **16** (© Bettmann), **17**
(© Bettmann), **18** (© Bettmann), **21** (© Robert Landau),
26 (epa/© Andreas Gebert); Getty Images pp. **5** (Digital
Vision/Rayman), **10** (Archive Photos/Authenticated
News), **12** (Hulton Archive/Imagno), **14** (Hulton
Archive/Rischgitz), **19** (American Stock Archive), **25**
(AFP Photo/Leon Neal), **27** (3D Systems Corp.); Image
supplied by Document Services, University of South
Australia p. **24**; Mary Evans Picture Library p. **9**; The Art
Archive p. **6** (The British Library); Xerox p. **22**.

Cover photograph of printing the *Colorado Star Journal*
newspaper, Pueblo, Colorado (c. 1910), reproduced with
permission of Corbis/© Bettmann.

We would like to thank Joan Boudreau for her invaluable
help in the preparation of this book.

Every effort has been made to contact copyright holders
of material reproduced in this book. Any omissions will
be rectified in subsequent printings if notice is given to
the publisher.

Disclaimer
All the Internet addresses (URLs) given in this book
were valid at the time of going to press. However, due
to the dynamic nature of the Internet, some addresses
may have changed, or sites may have changed or
ceased to exist since publication. While the author
and publisher regret any inconvenience this may cause
readers, no responsibility for any such changes can be
accepted by either the author or the publisher.

CONTENTS

Look for these boxes

Any words appearing in the text in bold, **like this**, are explained in the glossary.

Biographies

These boxes tell you about the life of inventors, the dates when they lived, and their important discoveries.

Setbacks

Here we tell you about the experiments that didn't work, the failures, and the accidents.

EUREKA!

These boxes tell you about important events and discoveries, and what inspired them.

TIMELINE

2011—The timeline shows you when important discoveries and inventions were made.

Think of all the books, magazines, and newspapers in your home and school, or in stores and libraries. All of the words and images they contain were produced using machines called printing presses.

Early books

Before printing presses were invented, books had to be written by hand. The earliest "books" were written 4,500 years ago. Unlike books today, they were scrolls made from rolled-up thin animal skin or rough paper.

Around 2,000 years ago, ancient Romans began to make books that were more like the books we use today. They were called codexes. A codex had several pages tied together along one edge, making the book easier to read.

Early books took months or years to write by hand. This meant they were rare and expensive.

4

2500 BCE—The earliest known writing on papyrus paper scroll is made

The products of printing presses contain huge amounts of knowledge, filling bookstores and libraries around the world.

An important invention

The invention of the printing press changed the world. After printed books appeared, more people could learn to read and write. Different inventions meant books could be made more quickly and cheaply. This meant more people could afford to buy them. The writings of scientists, scholars, poets, playwrights, and novelists could gradually spread worldwide.

As with most other important inventions, the printing press was not thought up by one person all at once. The invention of the printing presses we use today involved many inventors along the way.

EUREKA!

In 2010 the Internet company Google estimated that there were 129 million different book titles in existence at that time! Today, there are even more.

200 CE—The first codex books with several pages are made in ancient Rome

620 CE—Printed paper scrolls are made in China (see page 6)

868 CE—The oldest surviving printed scroll is made (see page 6)

around 1045—Bi Sheng invents the first **movable type** (see page 8)

The first prints

People have been printing for over 4,000 years. The earliest objects used for printing were probably carved stones. People pressed the stones into soft clay to leave copies of the carvings. Sometimes carved symbols were printed into clay around storeroom doors to say who owned what was inside. Symbols were also carved onto pieces of clay to give to others, like business cards are used today.

The earliest printed paper scrolls are thought to have been made around 620 CE in China, during the Tang Dynasty. The prints were made using carved blocks of wood.

This rare printed scroll from 868 CE survived in a Chinese desert cave until its discovery in 1900. It survived because the dry air stopped the paper from rotting.

1377—The first book printed with metal **movable type** is created in Korea (see page 8)

Woodblock printing

Early printers took pages that were handwritten on one side of thin paper. They stuck them back to front onto blocks of wood. Then they carved through the paper, removing the wood between the **characters** (letters and symbols). This left a **woodblock** of raised characters, called **type**, that was dipped in ink and printed onto paper. Italian explorer Marco Polo is said to have learned about woodblock printing when traveling in China in the 1200s. However, no one is sure whether or not this is how knowledge of printing spread to Europe.

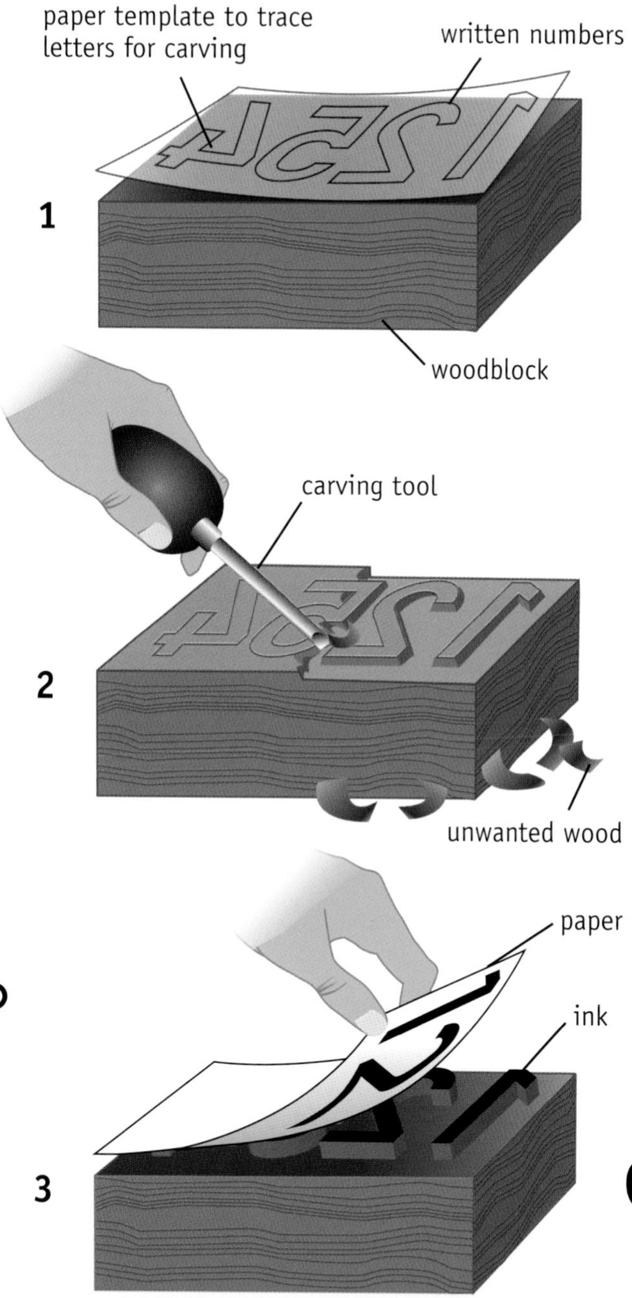

These are the main stages in woodblock printing.

paper template to trace letters for carving

written numbers

1

woodblock

carving tool

2

unwanted wood

paper

ink

3

Reusable type

Making woodblocks took a long time and could only be used for one book, because all the characters were carved together. Around 1045 Korean printer Bi Sheng invented **movable type** that could be reused. He carved individual characters into damp clay blocks, called type, and baked them. Then he arranged the type into words and fixed them into a **printing form**, using sticky wax. After printing from this form, Bi Shen heated the wax to unstick the type for use in different books.

This typesetter is picking wooden movable type from trays to make up a printing form.

The first metal type

Around 300 years later in Korea, in 1377, a female priest named Myodeok and her helpers printed the first books using metal movable type. The metal blocks were tougher than the clay ones, and they printed clearer characters.

8

1440—Johann Gutenberg invents his wooden press, which uses movable metal type (see page 10)

1440—The first Bibles printed using movable type are produced by Gutenberg (see page 10)

Metal plates

In **medieval** times, artists carved woodblocks to make printed images, but around 1430 they started to make metal **printing plates**. They used sharp tools to scratch images into the metal or into wax coating the metal. The metal dissolved in a liquid called acid wherever the wax had been scratched away. These **engraving** techniques could create much thinner lines and more detail than woodblocks. Also, the metal did not wear down as quickly during printing. Engraved printing plates are still used today for printing some things, such as paper money.

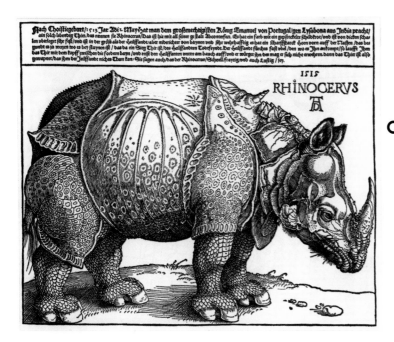

Some artists, such as Albrecht Dürer, became famous for their detailed engravings.

Setbacks

Whereas the English language uses around 300 characters, Chinese and Korean use tens of thousands of characters! Unfortunately this meant it took almost as long to **typeset** pages as it would to have carved woodblocks.

Around 1440, in Germany, Johann Gutenberg invented a printing press that used **movable type**. It took him the next 15 years to perfect the machine. In 1455 he used it to create the first Bibles printed using this method. Today, these are known as Gutenberg Bibles.

Gutenberg's printing press was fairly simple to use.

Smart inventor

It is thought that Gutenberg may have adapted some old technology to make his revolutionary invention. For example, his press had a handle that was turned on a wooden screw to force a wooden plate down. This worked like an olive press, but instead of squeezing oil from olives, it pressed **type** covered in ink onto paper! Gutenberg also used his own new ideas. He invented an improved **printing form** to hold the type blocks in place when printing pages, as well as a new way to make type.

1501—The first printed music is produced

1501—There are 1,000 print shops in Europe, printing 35,000 titles (see page 14)

1480

1500

Although a Gutenberg Bible was very expensive, it cost far less than a handwritten Bible.

Making type

Gutenberg made hard steel tools with letter shapes at the end. He hammered the tools into soft copper to make letter-shaped **molds**. Then he **cast** metal type by pouring hot, liquid metal into the molds and leaving it to cool and harden. One reason that Gutenberg's method was so popular was that printers could easily and quickly cast all sorts of **characters** using his technique.

Johann Gutenberg *(around 1400–1468)*

Johann Gutenberg was born in Mainz, Germany. His father was a merchant who paid for local priests to educate his son. Gutenberg worked for his father, but he also learned how to make fine gold jewelry and metal souvenirs that were sold to visitors in his local cathedral. His metalworking skills would prove useful in creating metal type.

Around the same time Gutenberg was making metal souvenirs, he had the idea of casting metal type to print pages of religious messages on paper. He did this because he knew they would be quicker to make and sell than the souvenirs. However, Gutenberg was not rich enough to open a printing shop, so he borrowed large amounts of money from a businessman named Johann Fust. Just when Gutenberg finally started to use movable type in a printing press, Fust demanded his money back. Gutenberg had to give his printing press and print shop to Fust to pay off his debt. Gutenberg struggled to repay the money, but he continued printing after setting up other print shops. However, it was Fust who became rich from selling the first printed Bibles.

Spreading technology

Gutenberg's movable type printing press was a success, and the technology spread. Historical records show that by around 1500 there were around 1,000 printers across Europe, all using similar printing machines. Printed books about mathematics, art, and many other topics, as well as printed music and newspapers, all appeared over the next centuries. Bookstores opened in cities.

This engraving shows a scene from a busy printing press in the 1500s.

Making copies

Some books were so popular that they were reprinted once the first batch had sold out. To save **typesetting** whole books again, William Ged invented **stereotypes** in 1725. These are cast metal copies of whole typeset printing forms for each page of a book. The molds were made by pressing clay onto the form.

1605—The first printed newspaper is produced in Germany

Spreading ideas

As it became easier to own or use printed books and papers, more people learned to read. New ideas spread fast. For example, up until the 1700s, North America was ruled by the British. American printing presses helped to spread the idea of independence from British rule.

This pamphlet was printed in 1776, to spread ideas during the Revolutionary War.

COMMON SENSE:

ADDRESSED TO THE

INHABITANTS

OF

AMERICA.

On the following interesting

SUBJECTS.

I. Of the Origin and Design of Government in general, with concise Remarks on the English Constitution.

II. Of Monarchy and Hereditary Succession.

III. Thoughts on the present State of American Affairs.

IV. Of the present Ability of America, with some miscellaneous Reflections.

Written by an ENGLISHMAN.

By Thomas Paine

Man knows no Master save creating HEAVEN,
Or those whom choice and common good ordain.

THOMSON.

PHILADELPHIA, Printed.
And Sold by R. BELL, in Third-Street, 1776.

Clementina Rind (1740–1774)

In 1773 Clementina Rind was the first female editor of an American newspaper called the *Virginia Gazette*. She printed many pieces opposing British rule, such as Thomas Jefferson's "A Summary View of the Rights of British America." Reading the pieces made people join the fight for independence, leading to the Revolutionary War (1775–83).

During the Industrial Revolution in the 1700s and 1800s, more and more work was carried out by machines powered by steam engines rather than by people.

Printing more

The first iron printing press was made by Earl Stanhope around 1800. Iron presses could print onto larger sheets of paper than wooden presses could. This is because more force is needed to push ink onto a large area than a small one, and weaker wooden presses could break! Printers could now produce many copies of large newspapers for the public.

A German printer named Friedrich Koenig invented the first steam-powered printing press in 1811. It could print almost four times as many sheets per hour as Gutenberg's hand-operated press.

Steam-powered printing presses allowed small numbers of workers to print many pages quickly, so books and newspapers became cheaper to buy.

Faster press

Printing speed improved further in 1847, when the American Richard Hoe invented the "Lightning Press." Hoe wanted to find a quicker alternative to printing sheets of paper one by one on a flat **printing form**. So he attached printing **type** to a large cylinder that was coated in ink using rollers. Hoe later improved his invention to print on rolls of paper rather than on separate sheets of paper. The machine would also automatically fold printed sheets. Hoe's Lightning Press could print 8,000 sheets per hour!

Setbacks

The lightning press was efficient, but it could be dangerous. If type on its revolving cylinder was not locked in tightly, it shot out like bullets when the press started turning!

Here, Richard Hoe displays one of his new presses to the public in the 1850s.

17

1710—Jacob Le Blon invents printing in color using four separate **printing plates** (see page 24)

Quicker pages

The slowest part of using printing presses was **typesetting** lines of **characters** by hand. However, typesetting became automatic with the arrival of **hot metal** machines. In 1884 Ottomar Mergenthaler invented one of these, called the Linotype machine. An operator typed lines of words on the Linotype keyboard. This formed rows of **molds** of the letters forming the line. Then hot, melted metal squirted into the molds to **cast** metal lines of type. The Linotype machines stacked lines of type beside each other to prepare pages for printing.

Here, an operator is typing words into a Linotype machine.

EUREKA!

Mergenthaler got the idea for the metal type molds from wooden molds that he had carved as a boy to make German Christmas cookies!

1725—William Ged invents **stereotyping** (see page 14)

Printing photos

In the mid-1800s, printing presses could only print photo images as solid black, rather than different shades of gray. For many newspapers and books, artists carved copies of photos onto **woodblocks** to print clearer photo images. In the 1880s, U.S. inventor Frederic Ives developed the **halftone** process to print using the original photos. He re-photographed photos through a checkered screen to turn the image into a pattern of small and large dots. This pattern was then **engraved** on metal **printing plates**. The dot pattern appeared as shades of gray when printed on paper.

Photos in newspapers showed people, places, and events that readers would have found hard to imagine before.

Ives failed to get a **patent** (official proof of invention) for his halftone idea. Then many other people used the idea without having to pay money to Ives!

Saving plates

Although metal printing plates are hard, they gradually wear down with the pressure of the press against the plate. The powerful, fast printing presses of the late 1800s made plates wear away quickly. In 1904 Ira Rubel found a solution. He added a cylinder covered in rubber called the "blanket." Greasy ink on the cylinder plate was transferred onto the blanket, and this then printed onto paper. The soft surface did not damage the plate. Rubel's system is called **offset printing**.

This diagram shows how an offset printing machine works.

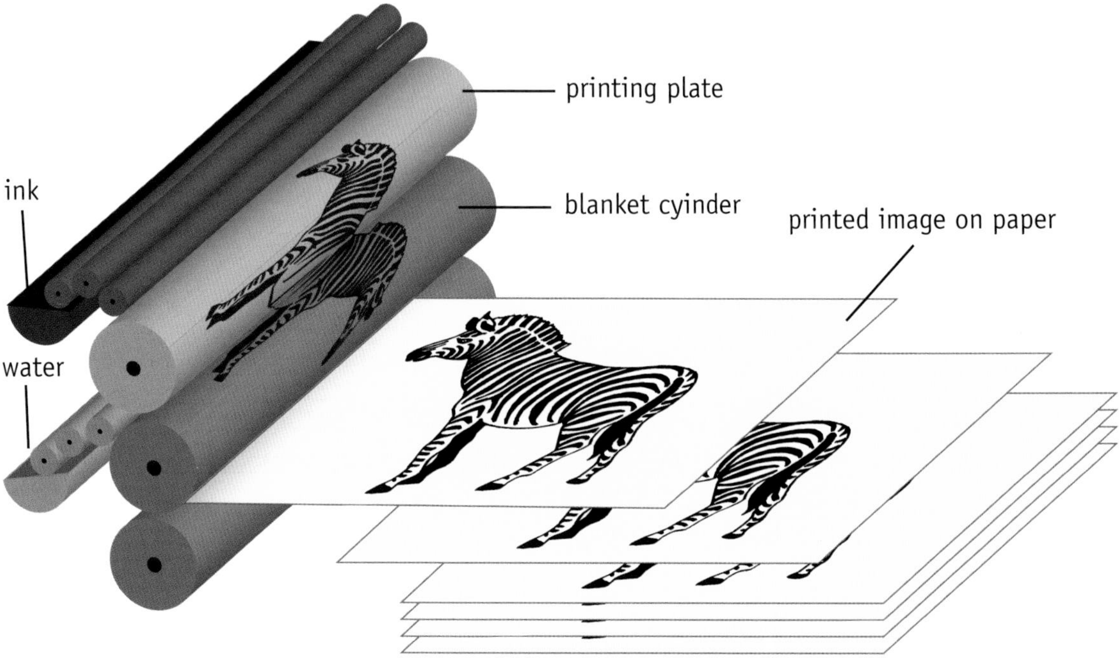

printing plate

ink

blanket cyinder

printed image on paper

water

Printing using light

Photographic film is coated with chemicals that change to a darker color where light hits it. In the early 1900s, many inventors tried to develop **photosetting** (using light and film for typesetting) because it would be cheaper and cleaner than hot metal.

Photosetting made it easier to make characters in large sizes, to be printed on things such as advertising posters.

The Photon

Louis Moyroud and René Higonnet invented the first practical photosetting machine in 1946. It was called the Photon. A transparent disc inside the machine was covered with letters, numbers, and other characters. Pressing keyboard keys rotated (turned) the disk to place different characters next to a light. Light shone through the disk to make the character shapes form on photographic film. Then light was used to transfer pages of type on film onto flat printing plates coated with light-sensitive chemicals.

PRINTING FROM COMPUTERS

Today—at home or school—many of us are used to printing directly from computers. American Gary Starkweather had the idea for a laser printer in 1967. But he was told by his company to stop working on the idea because lasers (machines that make bright light) were too expensive! Nevertheless, Starkweather continued in secret until he succeeded in 1971.

The printer Starkweather invented uses laser light to shine an image in the shape of **characters** onto a cylinder. Ink powder, called toner, sticks to the image like a magnet. The cylinder then rolls the toner onto paper, and the toner is heated to make it soak in, creating a printed page.

This was one of the first laser printers. It is much larger than the ones we have today!

1847—Richard Hoe invents the "Lightning Press" (see page 17)

1840   1860

Drops of ink

The other main type of personal printer is the ink-jet printer, invented in 1977 by Ichiro Endo. This is far simpler. A computer sends information to the printer. This makes a part called the print head move rapidly over the paper, line by line. The head fires out patterns of tiny ink droplets—no wider than a human hair—that form the characters on sheets of paper.

Japanese scientist Ichiro Endo was trying to figure out how to make a printer that fired ink out. He accidentally held a plastic syringe filled with ink against a hot iron. This created a bubble in the syringe that made ink squirt out. It was the inspiration behind the ink-jet printer!

An ink-jet printer heats ink inside the print head.

print head

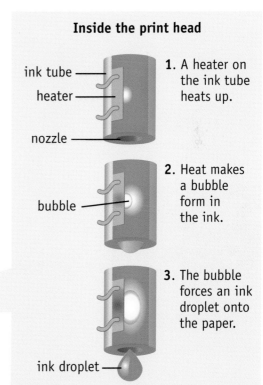

Inside the print head

ink tube

heater

nozzle

1. A heater on the ink tube heats up.

bubble

2. Heat makes a bubble form in the ink.

3. The bubble forces an ink droplet onto the paper.

ink droplet

23

1884—Ottomar Mergenthaler invents the Linotype machine (see page 18)

1888—Frederic Ives perfects the **halftone** process for printing photos (see page 19)

1880   1900

Color printing

The earliest color in printed books was added by hand to the black printed characters. In 1457 Johann Fust experimented with printing in two colors using **woodblocks** dipped in colored ink.

Around 1710 Jacob Le Blon invented four-color printing. This was a method of printing any color by overprinting yellow, blue, red, and black ink on the same sheet of paper using slightly different **printing plates**. It is like mixing colors on the paper. However, it was difficult to make the separate plates needed for printing a color photo. This finally changed in 1969, when inventor John Crosfield created the first color scanning machine. It used special color-sensitive sensors to recognize the different colors and separate them automatically.

cyan   magenta   yellow   black

Today, most images are printed using these four colors.

final image   close-up view of image

1904—Ira Rubel
invents **offset printing**
(see page 20)

1900   1920

Desktop publishing

During the 1960s, publishing companies started using computers to control **photosetting** machines. Most of these machines created lines of **type** that then had to be cut up and stuck into pages by hand. The problem was that this was very time-consuming. In 1984 Bob Doyle invented the first **desktop publishing** system. Using this computer software, people could design and **typeset** complete pages. In many printing factories today, desktop publishing systems can also be used to make printing plates.

In 2007 the Espresso Book Machine was set up in the New York Public library. It was the first machine that could carry out desktop publishing, print out pages, and glue them together into finished books!

The Espresso Book Machine, set up here in a bookstore, can print a book in five minutes.

1946—Moyroud and Higonnet invent the Photon photosetting machine (see page 21)

1940   1960

Today, thanks to computers, we can view words and images displayed on screens, as well as printed in ink on paper. The sales of printed newspapers are falling, because people can read up-to-date news on the Internet. People communicate their ideas in an instant using emails and social networking websites such as Facebook, rather than printing them.

Many people still prefer to read printed books. However, this has been changing since 1971, when U.S. scientist Michael Hart set up Project Gutenberg. This project stores books on a large computer for others to freely access and read. By 2010 there were over 33,000 books in Project Gutenberg, and many more electronic books were for sale.

In the future, will you read your favorite authors' works on a hand-held computer such as an iPad or Kindle, or in a printed book?

1969—John Crosfield invents the first machine that can make color **printing plates** automatically (see page 24)

1971—Gary Starkweather invents the laser printer. Michael Hart sets up Project Gutenberg. Ray Tomlinson invents email.

1977—Ichiro Endo invents the ink-jet printer (see page 23)

1984—Bob Doyle invents **desktop publishing** (see page 25)

1960

1980

Rachel Zimmerman

Rachel Zimmerman was 12 when she invented communication software for people who cannot easily speak or write. The person points to symbols on a touchscreen, and Rachel's Blissymbol Printer program translates the symbols into written language. This can be printed out or emailed in an instant.

A different way of printing

Some of today's printing presses can print solid objects! Three-dimensional (3D) printers are machines that print thin layers of special powders one by one on top of each other. The layers are heated until they harden, and they gradually build up to 3D shapes. Do you think that in the future we might print out objects for daily use, such as toys or spoons?

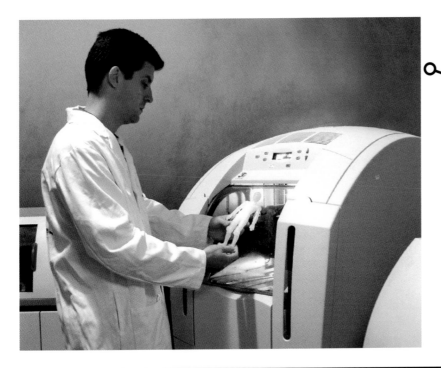

This 3D printer is very different from Gutenberg's printing press, but both inventions allow people to make accurate copies of ideas and information for others to see.

1990—Tim Berners-Lee invents the World Wide Web (Internet)

2010—The Apple iPad is released

TIMELINE

2500 BCE
The earliest known writing on papyrus paper scroll is made

around 200 BCE
The first codex books with several pages are made in ancient Rome

620 CE
Printed paper scrolls are made in China

1800
Lord Stanhope invents the iron printing press

1725
William Ged invents **stereotyping**

1710
Jacob Le Bron invents printing in color using four separate **printing plates**

1811
Friedrich Koenig invents a steam-powered printing press

1847
Richard Hoe invents the "Lightning Press"

1886
Ottomar Mergenthaler invents the Linotype machine

2010
The Apple iPad is released

1990
Tim Berners-Lee invents the World Wide Web (Internet)

1984
Bob Doyle invents **desktop publishing**

868 CE
The oldest surviving printed scroll is made

around 1045
Bi Sheng invents the first **movable type**

1377
The first book printed with metal movable type is created in Korea

1605
The first printed newspaper is produced in Germany

1501
There are 1,000 print shops in Europe, printing 35,000 titles. The first printed music is produced.

1440
Johann Gutenberg invents a wooden press that uses movable metal type. Bibles printed using movable type are made.

1888
Frederic Ives perfects the **halftone** process for printing photos

1904
Ira Rubel invents **offset printing**

1946
Moyroud and Higonnet invent the Photon **photosetting** machine

1977
Ichiro Endo invents the ink-jet printer

1971
Gary Starkweather invents the laser printer. Michael Hart sets up Project Gutenberg. Ray Tomlinson invents email.

1969
John Crossfield invents the first machine that can make color printing plates automatically

GLOSSARY

cast shaped form made by pouring hot metal (or wax) into a mold

character written or printed letter, number, or symbol

desktop publishing design, typeset, and lay out a book or other publication for printing on a computer

engrave carve or cut a design or letters into a hard material such as wood or metal

halftone printed image in which shades of color have been changed into dots of different sizes

hot metal system using an automatic machine for typesetting by casting with melted metal

medieval describing something that happened between the 400s and 1400s CE

mold hollow shape into which a fluid or soft substance is placed, to create a particular shape when it hardens

movable type separate pieces of type that can be put together individually into groups, forming a printing surface

offset printing common way of printing in which ink from a printing plate is transferred to a soft cylinder blanket, and from this to paper or another surface

patent official proof that an invention, idea, or process was the idea of a particular person, and protection from it being copied

photosetting typesetting in which character shapes are formed photographically using light

printing form frame into which typeset words and illustrations are arranged, in order to use to print pages

printing plate engraved thin sheet of metal, plastic, or other material used to transfer ink in the shape of images onto other surfaces

stereotype exact copy of a typeset printing form

type small metal or wooden block with a raised surface in the shape of a character, used for printing

typeset arrange type into words, lines, and pages ready for printing

woodblock block of wood with a carved design on the surface for printing

FIND OUT MORE

Books

Mullins, Lisa. *Inventing the Printing Press* (*Breakthrough Inventions*). New York: Crabtree, 2007.

Rees, Fran. *Johannes Gutenberg: Inventor of the Printing Press* (*Signature Lives*). Minneapolis: Compass Point, 2006.

Tames, Richard. *The Printing Press: A Breakthrough in Communication* (*Point of Impact*). Chicago: Heinemann Library, 2006.

Websites

www.historyforkids.org/learn/literature/printing.htm
This history of printing includes a video of someone creating a woodblock print.

www.ondemandbooks.com/video2.htm
Learn more about the Espresso Book Machine (see page 25) at this website, which features a video about the machine.

http://interactives.mped.org/view_interactive.aspx?id=110&title
Visit this website to make and print out your own newspaper or booklet.

Places to visit

The Museum of Printing History
1324 W. Clay Street
Houston, Texas 77019
www.printingmuseum.org

The International Printing Museum
315 W. Torrance Boulevard
Carson, California 90745
www.printmuseum.org

INDEX